Made in the USA
Columbia, SC
24 May 2022

60877344R00067